I Feel Sad

Written by Brian Moses

Illustrated by Mike Gordon

sundance

A Haights Cross Communications ✦ Company

Kid-to-Kid Books

Red Set	Green Set	Blue Set	Yellow Set
I Feel Angry	I Feel Bored	I Feel Bullied	Excuse Me!
I Feel Happy	I Feel Jealous	I Feel Frightened	I Don't Care!
I Feel Lonely	I Feel Shy	I Feel Sad	I'll Do It!
It's Not Fair	I Feel Worried	Why Wash?	It Wasn't Me!

This edition published
in North America by
Sundance Publishing
P.O. Box 740
One Beeman Road
Northborough, MA 01532

First published in 1993 by
Wayland Publishers Limited

Copyright © 1993 Wayland Publishers Limited

ISBN 0-7608-3914-X

sundance ™
A Haights Cross Communications Company

Printed in China

In the corner today,
we're talking about

feeling sad.

This way to Kids Corner

3

When I feel sad, I feel like

a flower that
needs watering,

a rainbow that
has lost its colors,

a clown who
can't smile.

When I feel sad,
I lie on my bed
and I don't want
to talk to anyone.

I hide in my playhouse.

I cuddle my teddy.

SQUEEEEEK

7

All sorts of things make me feel sad. When my best friend moves far away, I feel sad.

I promise I'll write.

But it will be great
to get lots of letters!

When Spot is sick, and the vet says,
"He's getting very old,"

I feel sad.

But then I remember all the fun
we've had together.

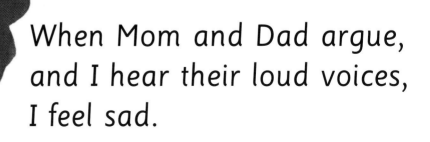

When Mom and Dad argue,
and I hear their loud voices,
I feel sad.

But the next day,
they're smiling and happy again.

When I say good-bye to Grandma,
and I know I won't see her
for a while,
we both feel sad.

So I give her an extra long hug,
and we both feel better!

When I'm the only one
not invited to a party,
I feel sad.

So I have a party for my toys instead!

When I paint a picture at school,
and then someone spoils it,
I feel sad and angry!

But next time,
I'll paint one that's
even better.

19

When I feel sad,
it helps if I tell my problems to Grandpa.

It helps if I do a jigsaw puzzle
or watch something funny on TV.

It helps if I have something
to look forward to.

It helps if I do something nice
for someone else.

Sometimes I make people feel sad—

like when I call
someone names,

or when I break
someone's toy.

If I say mean things,
it makes Mom or Dad feel sad.

If I won't play with a friend,
it makes him feel sad.

28

If you feel sad,
remember this—
a frown
is just a smile
turned upside down!

Things to Do in the Kids Corner

Trace your hand on oaktag and cut out the tracing. On each side, write a word that makes you feel happy, like *bubble gum* or *baseball*. Glue the oaktag hand to a stick. When you feel sad, you can "wave your sadness away!"

Make a "Sad-to-Glad Card." On an index card, write a list or draw pictures of things that make you happy. Keep the card with you. The next time you feel sad, look at your card and feel glad!

On a piece of paper, draw a tic-tac-toe grid and write *sad* in the center square. Fill in your grid by writing another *-ad* word in each of the other squares.

No wonder the rainbow on page 5 is sad—it has lost its colors! It's up to you to give them back. On a piece of drawing paper, draw a big, beautiful, colorful rainbow!

Make up a silly song that you could sing to cheer up someone who is sad. Teach your song to a friend.

Other Books to Read

Special Friends, by Wendy Body (a Sundance *Book Project* book, 1998). Four special friends share the same birthday. Together they go to the toy shop to choose their presents. The toys that the children want are the toymaker's favorites. He is sad to see his special toys go, but he knows that the toys and the children can make each other happy. *24 pages*

Looking for Dad, by Ellen Frances (Sundance, 1999). John is upset when his mom plans to marry Steve. But no one asks John how he feels. Looking for the perfect dad brings John disappointment and sadness. But his search has a surprising ending. *64 pages*

The Trouble with Parents, by Dianne Bates (Sundance, 1997). Craig and Sarah are really excited about Open House until they find out that their parents will not be coming. Not even old Mrs. Butler from next door or Aunty Lyn or Uncle Peter will be there. All the other kids will have visitors except them. The twins won't be sad for long, though. *64 pages*

Angel Child, Dragon Child, by Michele Maria Sturat, (Scholastic Books, 1989). Ut has just come to America from Vietnam without her mother. She misses her mother, and she does not like her new school. *35 pages*

Annie and the Old One, by Miska Miles, (Little, Brown & Company, 1971). Annie, a Navajo girl, refuses to believe that her grandmother is going to die. Annie finally faces the truth with acceptance. *44 pages*